CUSTER'S RECONNAISSANCE

by

Terrance E. Heitter

DORRANCE
PUBLISHING CO
EST. 1920
PITTSBURGH, PENNSYLVANIA 15238

Dorrance Publishing Co
585 Alpha Drive, Suite 103
Pittsburgh, PA 15238
Visit our website at *www.dorrancebookstore.com*

ISBN: 979-8-8852-7387-9
eISBN: 979-8-8852-7511-8

To my wife, Sandie, for her love, patience and professional input into this manuscript, plus a heck-of-a-lot of work.

CONTENTS

INTRODUCTION

What I am about to write stems from a lifetime of interest and personal feelings involving the 7th U.S. Cavalry and the Lakota and Cheyenne Indians at the Little Big Horn River in the Montana Territory in June of 1876. I have been to the Little Big Horn Battlefield National Monument on a number of occasions to study and enjoy what history it gives to us. I also belong to the 7th U.S. Cavalry Association, having voluntarily served with that regiment in combat in Vietnam 1968.

I have read and studied over 70 books regarding the Little Big Horn battle, all of which are in my private library, and have gone over numerous maps of the area. I believe that over this time period, I have achieved a very excellent opinion of what actually happened in that 1876 conflict with the roaming tribes of the Lakota and Cheyenne Native Americans and the 7th U.S. Cavalry in the U.S. Army 1876 Indian Expeditionary Force.

The battle of the Little Big Horn on June 25 & 26, 1876 in the Montana Territory between the 7th U.S. Cavalry and the roaming tribes of the Lakota and Cheyenne Native Americans is one of the most written about fights in American history. Even though it has been covered extensively, it still is the most mis-construed and mis-interpreted conflict. It still has not been explained with the truth of the facts, the whole truth. That is what I intend to do.

Through time, literature has focused on who to blame for the catastrophe and have been extremely biased in its written accounts for or against who gets the blame. Some people cannot accept the fact that the Indians won and the 7th U.S. Cavalry was defeated. The Lakota and Cheyenne were strong in resolve and numbers, and had the recent victory over General George Crook at the battle of the Rosebud on June 17th to give them confidence.

The authors of many Battle of the Little Big Horn books write with pre-established biases based on information accumulated with pre-conceived ideas from actual participants of the battle, and/or, participants who gave information based on leading questions from various researchers trying to get support for their own opinions. There also have been very good Battle of the Little Big Horn books written by knowledgeable, informed authors, researchers and historians who truly give reasonable accounts of their version of the battle, but are inaccurate or incomplete due to various reasons. The scenarios are endless and in many cases not even based on fact, reason or even common sense.

There probably have been at least a thousand different scenarios written as to where, what, why, when, how and who did what in the battle of the Little Big Horn. Many of the legends have reasonable substance and may in part be the truth, but most are biased either for or against LTC. Custer personally. Some of the ideas to what happened are totally out of context and seem to be written without any military combat knowledge or knowing of Indian fighting procedures. Also, many writings have had no semblance of the time - distance relationship to the terrain features. Some books have been written in such detail that they contained actual commentary between LTC. Custer and his subordinate officers who were all killed in the battle.

One thing that I find interesting is when different authors write about the battle of the Little Big Horn and spend enormous amounts of time and paper arguing over which coulee is the correct one taken from Weir Point, or which battalion Company C was assigned to, or getting involved with the misadventures of Crow scout Curly, or why did Custer wait 45 minutes at Luce Ridge, or what if Reno or Benteen did this instead of that. Too much has been written about insignificant or false ideas. The final results are indicated correctly by archeological findings, placement of the 7th U.S. Cavalry trooper's body locations and with logic and Indian commentary. The battle was not an all day affair with the cavalry making a number of major tactical maneuvers.

The fight was fast and simple in regards to the military exigencies.

Taking the time of day and placing the events when they occurred in sequence and combining the military exigencies of the battle with judgements of distance and terrain is important to understand the battle. Even thinking of ease of movement takes consideration.

Another discerning element in the Little Big Horn battle is what was the only known pre-information available to the leaders when they made decisions at given times, not information that was later known to be after the battle. The officers had fragmentary and very limited knowledge at their disposal when making important decisions.

Indian narratives are extremely important because they can show true substance where events happened as to where the events were thought to be located. They can show what routes the soldiers actually took versus where pre-determined routes were thought to be. The Indian narratives have given confirmation to a number of previously questionable events. The "5" company Custer fight is shown with extremely good reasoning as per the only live participant's personal views. The Indian accounts make sense when the Indians tell the story, because it's their personal view as they saw it in their limited vision. Taking all these individual visions and putting them together, gives a true account to an individual event. These facts will be presented in my quest to show the actual truths of the battle.

By combining information from my numerous sources, I will be able to present a very factual account of the Little Big Horn battle and it will run simply. I hope it will have some definite eye openings to those individuals who have pre-determined attitudes. What I will be saying will go along with the time - event process and should discuss what may seem to be not normally accepted ideas to already hardened believers.

I want to thank whole heartedly and give credit to some of the many authors whom I have used some information from their writings to which they dedicated an enormous amount of hard work and deep thinking. Their research has been invaluable to my evaluations and final conclusions.

The first author is Frederic C. Wagner III with his book, "The Strategy of Defeat at the Little Big Horn". His military and timing analysis of the battle is absolutely remarkable with all of the timelines of each event that took place during the fight. His dedication to facts is phenomenal. I do not agree with everything he has written, but his book has been invaluable to my thoughts using his devised format.

The second author is Roger Darling with his book, "A Sad and Terrible Blunder". This book is a masterpiece of research regarding the strategic side of the battle of the Little Big Horn. It takes in General Alfred Terry's role as the 1876 Indian Expedition Commander and shows the critical aspects of his involvement with the results of the battle against the Lakota and Cheyenne Indians and the fate of the 7th U.S. Cavalry Regiment. I have been awed at the value of this book, although I do not agree with it entirely. One thing that I like is that he stresses what information was really available to the leaders for them to make the decisions they did at the appropriate times.

The third author is Gregory F. Michno and his book, "Lakota Noon". This book involving the narratives of the actual Native American participants is an eye opener. It is the glue that puts the battle in the right perspective. It takes away numerous mistruths and irrational ideas and puts simple, authentic reasoning to the events of the battle. Yes, the Native American Lakota and Cheyenne are the only ones who could give the truths of the battle with the five companies of the 7th U.S. Cavalry under LTC. Custer. There are other important answers that have also been brought to light with their testimony. The author's dedication to real fact is unparalleled. He let the Indians tell their story in their own words.

I would recommend to all those persons interested in the Battle of the Little Big Horn to definitely procure these three books as "MUST READ" to really enhance their knowledge of the subject.

I have also included maps in this study in order to allow the reader a more clear picture of what I have written, these will be seen in Appendix 1.

CHAPTER 1:

"1876 Indian Expeditionary Force"

One aspect of the Little Big Horn battle has been totally eliminated by most of the authors and researchers who have been only concerned with the 7th U.S. Cavalry and mainly the demise of Custer's five companies on battle ridge. Little has been said about the 1876 Indian Expeditionary Force that the 7th U.S. Cavalry was part of and the role that it played which had repercussions to the 7th U.S. Cavalry defeat.

One must assess the overall strategic plan that the Battle of the Little Big Horn was part of, to which General Alfred Terry, commander of the 1876 Indian Expedition, was responsible. The Department of the Interior wanted all the roaming bands of Native American Indians rounded up and taken to the respective Indian agencies/reservations, with force if necessary. The first problem with that was that the U.S. Army did not have the resources or procedure to do it. There was no doctrine of Indian warfare developed to use against the hostile plains Indians. This definitely had an adverse effect on the success of the operation to subdue the Lakota and Cheyenne plains Indians. Also, the U.S. Army had no respect for the Indians as a fighting force strong enough to put up a challenge to the U.S. Cavalry, who were thought to be the force on the plains. The Native Americans did not allow themselves to do battle on conditions they believed to be unfavorable. The U.S. Army 1870's extant of the Lakota and Cheyenne had a racial arrogance about the Indians which spread down to the military field officers and troops. The 1876 campaign gave Generals Alfred Terry and

George Crook a lot of mental baggage to overcome. They were definitely concerned and obsessed that the Indians would run and flee from the troops, that they would not be caught.

General Philip H. Sheridan, the U.S. Army Division Commander, originated the overall 1876 Indian Expedition to subdue the roaming Native Americans. He had General George Crook with his command coming from Wyoming, Colonel John Gibbon with his combined infantry and cavalry command coming from Montana and General Alfred Terry with his command, including the 7th U.S. Cavalry, converging from the Dakotas to the Indian summer hunting grounds. One or more of these columns should be able to complete the mission. It was only an idea, not a coordinated effort. General Terry would be the senior officer in the field and the strategic field plan would be for him to devise. General Crook's column was a thorn in General Terry's plans. Crook was too far south to communicate with and he was really not concerned about what General Terry wanted from his column. He considered himself to be independent from Terry's command, but he was moving north to the target area. Unfortunately, on 17 June 1876, the Lakota and Cheyenne attacked his forces and sent General Crook's column reeling back southward from the Rosebud River. Crook did not relay this happening on to General Terry and it may have had an impact on the coming events had Terry known about that defeat, it would have made him much more cautious.

General Terry had made definite plans to overcome the roaming Lakota and Cheyenne Indians. The U.S. Army did know that there were a lot of Indians, but Terry had no hard facts on the Lakota and Cheyenne whereabouts to reach sound conclusions to base a well considered plan of attack. Some skilled scouts gave General Terry some information as to where the Indians might be located, looking to past gatherings and according to habits. The Indians roamed their hunting grounds according to where the game took them. Any direction was fair game to the roamers. The Indians traveled by tribes or circles, not always combining forces. In fact, the roaming Indians could split their march at any time, having the families going their separate ways.

General Terry or Lt. Colonel Custer had no defined target location and no defined number of villages or number of Indians. The current target seemed to be north of the Big Horn Mountains, east of the Big Horn River, south of the Yellowstone River and west of the Rosebud. Designing a battle plan was extremely difficult with the above total target area. (see map 1, appendix 1) General Terry's knowledge of the Indian hunting grounds was based on only two things. First was a chart assembled by two military engineers in the 1859-60 survey. It shows that the target was in an unexplored and unmapped region. This map only had the river and streams showing, no topography included.

The second source of information was from the scouts intelligence. General Terry made his strategic plans before making contact about the terrain from the Montana column's cavalry scouts, LT. Bradley and LT. Ball or LT. Mc Clernand, the engineering officer. This proved to be a very big mistake in the strategic plan against the hostile Indians. General Terry also did not aquaint himself with the Montana column's scouting abilities or their past scouting information, which included some of the possible target area where Terry thought the Indians might be presently located, that included the Little Big Horn area. Long range scouting took time, but LT. Bradley and his Crow scouts had done reconnaissance deep into the target area in the previous months. General Terry only sent Major Reno to scout for the roaming Lakota and Cheyenne Indians in an area that was not included in his final plan. Reno's scout did give Terry a possibly better general location to where hostiles might be, by eliminating most of the eastern square mileage, but that still left a tremendous territory untouched. General Terry had time on his side, the Indians were not going anywhere and he needed fresh operational intelligence. He should have sent out long range reconnaissance patrols to locate the hostiles. This was his responsibility as Expedition Commander and he definitely had the resources to accomplish that scouting necessity with the number of Indian (Ree & Crow) and white scouts. General Terry's failure of this duty might have been attributed to the fact that he wanted his plan implemented right away and he was also afraid that the hostiles would run and scatter before his plan could be fulfilled. The Indians were with their families, belongings and pony herds. How fast could they move? Encumbered with the above would also restrain the Indian's fighting abilities against the mobile cavalry.

General Terry could have contacted General Crook, found out about his battle and then Terry may have assumed a more cautious posture for his own column. General Terry had in mind that General Crook's Wyoming force could act as a "blocking force" while his Montana and Dakota columns would press the Indians to the south, having the Big Horn River (to which was Crow country on the west) to act as a funnel, whether Crook was aware of Terry's maneuver or not. I am sure it was discussed between General Terry and LTC. Custer about what the plan would be if Custer would come in contact with General Crook's Wyoming column in the southern part of the Indian target area.

General Terry had decided on his force structure of a double movement before defining his target. He assumed that his troops were stronger than any size force that the Indians would come up with to battle. General Terry did not employ a single column reconnaissance attack force of the combined 7th U.S. Cavalry and the Montana column cavalry (four companies of the 2nd U.S. Cavalry) and Infantry. Terry believed that either of his subordinate columns alone could prevail against any Indian target. A single column would keep the total strength intact until the target would become clearer and the troops could be maneuvered with close coordination.

General Terry's two column attack and blocking force plan divided the Expedition's strength and caused a problem of coordination of the two forces by distance and communication. Not knowing the location and size of the Indian force, put both the 7th U.S. Cavalry and the Montana column in a self supporting position for who would be the one to engage the Indians.

As previously noted, the map of the target area was created by several army engineer officers in 1859-60. Since that time, it was renamed the Hancock Map 1872. This map only had the rivers and some streams located and had no topography included. (see map 1, appendix 1) Therefore, General Terry and LTC. Custer were looking at unexplored terrain. Coordinated movements of the Montana and 7th U.S. Cavalry columns could only be estimated or assumed. The ground enclosed was 5,000 square miles. It was later found that the terrain from the Rosebud to the Little Big Horn River at the headwaters was very poor and would have given LTC. Custer problems had he gone that route which General Terry envisaged. General Terry found out the tremendous difficulties of the terrain from Tullock Creek to the Big Horn River when he decided to change his course from moving south up Tullock Creek on the way to the Little Big Horn River, delaying the movement of the Montana column to the mouth of the Little Big Horn, thereby canceling coordination with the 7th U.S. Cavalry. (see map 2, appendix 1)

The leadership of the 1876 Indian Expeditionary Force against the roaming tribes of the Lakota and Cheyenne seemed to be questionable from the start. General Terry, as the Department Commander, initially was to have Lt. Colonel Custer lead the entire expedition. Then, after Custer's problem with President Grant, Terry at least was allowed to have LTC. Custer as one of his subordinate officers and General Terry, himself, was to command the Expedition, a post that he definitely did not want. General Terry did want LTC. Custer to be his attack force leader, mainly having to do with Custer's western Indian experience and Terry's lack of the same. General Terry was confident of his own planning ability, but was indecisive of his own tactical ability for Indian warfare. The Terry - Custer relationship was questionable and in the end, LTC. Custer was given the attack force role without General Terry accompaning it. Terry decided to go with COL. Gibbon's Montana column which proved to be a disaster in the making.

General Terry discussed his complete strategic intentions verbally to LTC. Custer and COL. Gibbon on June 21st, 1876 at the riverboat conference the day before the 7th U.S. Cavalry started its expedition up the Rosebud and the Montana column started west on the Yellowstone. Later, LTC. Custer received written orders which were prepared by Captain E. W. Smith, Acting Assistant Adjutant General, and were intended as a written guide for General Terry's intentions of his plans. (see appendix 3)

The controversy about the written orders after LTC. Custer's death was made for the purpose of pointing the blame of the defeat on Custer, rather than implying General Terry had been part of the defeat. But that body of information they all verbally agreed to at the riverboat conference comprised Terry's complete plan. These written orders by

CPT. Smith to LTC. Custer were not the complete strategic intentions as discussed and approved by General Terry, LTC. Custer and COL. Gibbon on the Far West at the riverboat conference. The concise summary of General Terry's strategic plan involved a double movement of troops. The two columns would approach the Indian target area from different directions, hopefully, they would be within general cooperating distance from each other and to arrive there by late 25th of June, 1876. The 26th of June, each was to execute closing marches moving generally toward each other, keeping the Indians between the two columns.

The Lakota and Cheyenne were expected to be north of the Big Horn Mountains and east of the Big Horn River. Crow country was on the west side of the Big Horn River. LTC. Custer, in command of the attack force, would be ready to initiate his movement down the Little Big Horn River route on the 26th of June. He was expected to find and strike the Indian village first, assuming one was there, but it was also considered that the Montana column blocking force might be the first to strike the Indian village. LT. Bradley, COL. Gibbon's chief of scouts, on June 21st said "they had a conference on the boat and reveals that it is understood that if Custer arrives first to the Indian village, he is at the liberty to attack at once if he deems prudent and he will undoubtedly exert himself to get there and win all the laurels for himself and his regiment."

It should also be noted that LTC. Custer's route, as designed by General Terry, could have gone as far south as the Tongue headwaters. Also, LTC. Custer and the 7th U.S. Cavalry were to take care of any Indians to the east of the Rosebud. If either of the above situations happened, LTC. Custer's Regiment would be on its own with no support from the Montana column. No one knew where the Indians were actually located. Two columns covering that vast area would have been lucky to have had coordinated results, not knowing specifically where the hostiles were camped. The exact location of the so-called Indian target area could have been very far up the Little Big Horn River, not as far down as was found. (see map 1, appendix 1) There could have been many miles between the Montana column and the 7th U.S. Cavalry on the 25th & 26th of June. Gibbon's column could have possibly been alone in the Little Big Horn valley, and Custer wherever. Terry gave Custer wide discretion to implement his plan. With the possibilities of the Lakota and Cheyenne Indians moving to the east from the Rosebud, this being the case, it can readily be seen that absolute or definite instructions were about impossible. Custer needed the freedom to decide his course of action where ever the target would be. Also, the facts were, as seen by the Crow and Ree scouts, that besides a lot of Indians there were numerous circles and tribes who were relying on wherever the game would be to feed their families. The hostiles did not know where they would be on any given day. There was no notification from other tribes to join up at any specific location at any specific date. It was not always beneficial to the numerous circles to consolidate.

General Terry with his pre-established thoughts (extant of the plains Indians) believed that either one of his columns would defeat the Lakota and Cheyenne forces by itself. He hoped that one of the two columns would find them. He dispatched this opinion to General Sheridan.

On 22 June 1876, General Alfred Terry put his two columns, the Montana column heading west along the Yellowstone and the 7th U.S. Cavalry moving southward along the Rosebud, in action to advance into the roaming Lakota and Cheyenne hunting grounds in order to subdue the Indians and return them to various reservations/Indian agencies.

General Terry, as Expedition Commander, chose to accompany the Montana column, commanded by Colonel Gibbon, and made it clear that this role suited him. The subordinate officers would be the ones to plan and command the actual fighting. The Montana column and the riverboat Far West were headed toward the mouth of Tullock Creek, just south of the Yellowstone River. On the night of the 23rd of June, COL. Gibbon was struck down with a severe illness and he was confined to bed. Now, General Terry was faced with giving the command of the Montana column to Major Brisbin alone or to take the dual command of the Montana column and the Expeditionary force by himself. General Terry was extremely proud and confident of his strategic plan, but could he jeopordize its success to Major Brisbin to command the blocking force. Terry decided he would accompany the Montana column and give Brisbin an honorary command role with himself being the real commander. This was to neither one's liking, for various reasons.

CHAPTER 2:

"MONTANA COLUMN ADVANCE"

On the early morning of June 24th, the riverboat Far West stopped on the Yellowstone River and began to shuttle the Montana column from the northside to the southside of the river. It was late morning before General Terry sent over the Crow scouts who were to recon Tullock Creek and he did not send LT. Bradley, the chief of scouts, or any white scouts to accompany them. This was just the beginning of the many mistakes made by Terry and his officers that day. (see map 2, appendix 1)

The crossing was a comedy of errors, inefficiency at it's finest, a total waste of hours that could have moved the Montana column toward the Little Big Horn according to General Terry's strategic plan requirements and timing. The Crow scouts, if they had been the first to cross the Yellowstone as they should have by far-sighted planning, could have been miles up the Tullock valley.

Now, it would be dark by the time General Terry would receive the benefit of the Crow scouts information. Later, Terry did send LT. Bradley ahead to find a campsite for the night at the mouth of Tullock Creek. This decision was critical concerning the success of the Indian Expeditionary Force. A forced march down the Tullock valley that afternoon would put the Montana column in a much better position to allow for success. General Terry was also concerned about receiving George Herendeen, from LTC. Custer's column, with information on the Tullock headwaters and route north. The Montana column was to move up the Tullock Creek so as to encounter Herendeen. The Crow scouts had not yet returned from their reconnaissance up Tullock Creek. General Terry decided to camp rather than continue on, knowing it was a questionable thing to do. He was not used to command decisions at this level.

General Terry now could see one of the errors of his strategic plan. Close coordination was not possible, whatever coordination might be achieved would be most likely accidental. The fact was, that mileage distances on a deficient map were only estimates at best and trying to maneuver two columns separated by many miles was only a guess for coordination purposes. General Terry and the Montana column were a day behind of the closing-action time already. The Crow scouts returned without any information, as they only went south on Tullock Creek a few miles from the Yellowstone. Yes, the 24th of June, 1876 was a wasted day. (see map 2, appendix 1)

No communication from George Herendeen probably meant that hostiles were on Tullock Creek. General Terry needed to know if the Indians were there. The absence of intelligence was now most important. On the 25th of June, he would have many additional miles to travel to keep with the Expedition schedule. Here, General Terry is required to implement his leadership by moving the Montana column along with his own Expedition operational plan. Terry was wearing two hats. One was the Montana column hat and the second was his Indian Expeditionary Force hat. He wasn't pleased with either, let alone both. So, on the 25th of June, Terry sent off a detachment of Crow scouts by themselves and another detachment of Crow scouts with LT. Bradley in charge to move south on Tullock Creek and hoping to contact LTC. Custer or scout George Herendeen.

According to General Terry's orders, LTC. Custer was to make a reconnaissance of Tullock Creek headwaters in the south. The Montana column would check out the north end. Tullock Creek was off to the northwest of Custer's route, but General Terry gave LTC. Custer a scout, George B. Herendeen, to traverse the Tullock and then take that information to the Montana column or Terry, himself.

On the morning of June 24th, LTC. Custer called for George Herendeen as the 7th U.S. Cavalry was heading south on the Rosebud. Custer told Herendeen at this time to scout out the Tullock Creek headwaters and continue on to General Terry with the information. Custer even told Herendeen to take along another white scout, Charlie Reynolds, with him. George Herendeen told LTC. Custer that the gap leading to Tullock Creek was still further ahead and he would continue scouting for Custer until the time came when he needed to check out the Tullock Creek headwaters. Later in the day, George Herendeen went to and told LTC. Custer that they had reached the gap leading to the Tullock Creek area. Custer then made no response back to Herendeen, but just looked at him; with Herendeen just falling back in column and not making his ride to Tullock Creek and General Terry. "Why" is the big question. LTC. Custer at this time was receiving many reports from his scouts to the location of hostile Indian sign and it was late in the day. Custer had a lot on his mind and Herendeen's mention of Tullock Creek was just an unconcerned nuisance. Herendeen did not need to ask, he just needed to go and do his assigned job. Maybe Herendeen, knowing that there was a chance for attacking the hostiles who were really close now, didn't want to miss the battle. Who knows? LTC. Custer told George Herendeen to go earlier, he didn't have to tell Herendeen twice. For the record, this failure to get the results of the Tullock Creek's scout to General Terry was possibly a major drawback to General Terry's success for the Indian Expeditionary Force and that was the only information General Terry required from scout George Herendeen, no information was necessary from LTC. Custer.

LT. Mc Clernand, an engineer officer who had participated in a scouting mission with LT. Ball of the Montana column about a month previous in this area, was given the lead for General Terry's column to move south in the Tullock valley. (see map 2, appendix 1)

On the 25th of June, the Montana column march started out reasonably well, but General Terry had not planned his march with any advice from his scouts, either white men or Indian, and he knew that time and distance was most important. Terry was reluctant to get advice from the Native American Crow scouts. After the march had gone off a few miles, the white scout, Hamilton Taylor, who had no experience in this area, talked General Terry into changing the route to save time and miles. The Crow scouts and LT. Mc Clernand were knowledgeable about this terrain, but were left out of this decision which ended up being the deciding fatal mistake for Terry.

The facts of the deficiencies of the alternate route was horrible for the troops and General Terry. The Montana column led off to the right, southward, and was intending to proceed to the Little Big Horn River mouth. (see map 2, appendix 1) The new route ordered by General Terry, on his own decision, had LT. Mc Clernand ascend the Tullock divide and head for the Little Big Horn mouth. The day was hot and the terrain began to rise with the infantrymen and cavalrymen climbing up the slopes. There was no water to be had at this elevation and the troops' canteens were emptied early. The men were totally exhausted and, unfortunately, this was only the beginning of the day. The column was now lost in a maze of coulees, attempting to reach the Big Horn River, since it was the closest water. LT. Bradley with his scouts way up the Tullock valley, was wondering where the main column had gone. When Bradley found out from some of Terry's cavalry, he was shocked. He managed to backtrack and find the Montana column. What he saw was infantrymen mixed in with cavalrymen and their horses, mules and equipment were all confined in crooked, narrow ravines. These men were looking at survival, the situation was entirely unspeakable. There was not a cohesive battle-ready blocking force any longer. Eventually, they made it to the Big Horn River and the necessary water. This was another spike in the success of the 1876 Indian Expedition. The two hats that General Terry was wearing, both succumbed to failure. It left the Montana column out of the picture for the Expedition's success. This left General Terry's column approximately 20 miles from the mouth of the Little Big Horn, a day behind his closing-action time. It left LTC. Custer with no support if needed, the 7th U.S. Cavalry was by itself. (see map 2, appendix 1)

CHAPTER 3:

"7TH U.S. CAVALRY ADVANCE"

After the 7th U.S. Cavalry left General Terry and the Gibbon column at the Yellowstone River junction with the Rosebud River, it moved south with the regiment intact and operating with proper military procedures looking for the trail of the hostile Lakota and Cheyenne forces. The reconnaissance at this time was led by LT. Varnum and the Ree Indian scouts and Mitch Boyer and his six Crow scouts. (see map 2, appendix 1) During the several day journey south along the Rosebud River, Custer was adamant about watching for hostile Indian sign. He did not want to miss any sign however small and especially for any sign to the east. What came to fruition was a lot of Indian movement, but no sign of movement east. There were many converging signs to add to the already massive Indian movement to the intersection of the Rosebud River and Davis Creek at Busby. Here, the hostiles went west toward the Little Big Horn and the massive trails and hostile encampments were huge. From Busby, there was no sign of the hostile Indians moving to the south along the Rosebud.

LTC. Custer and his scouts had been riding ahead of the command. The Crows told Custer about the Lakota crossing the Rosebud divide and leading to the Little Big Horn. They also told Custer that he could view the Little Big Horn valley when it got light. The prospect of an earlier awareness as to the hostile's position - if they should be in the Little Big Horn valley - now prompted LTC. Custer to cancel his plan to stay the night in his present position and instead to proceed in a night march toward the divide.

General Terry's orders gave LTC. Custer the freedom to make the best decisions. LTC. Custer had two alternatives: First was to take General Terry's recommendation, which was to be a two day circle to the headwaters of the Little Big Horn River and then proceed up the river toward COL. Gibbon's blocking force, hoping the Indians remained stationary; The second was to march that night under the cover of darkness to a point near the Rosebud divide where the regiment could lay concealed the next day while the scouts pinpointed the location of the Indian village. He could then make a night approach and launch the surprise attack at dawn of the 26th. Both of these alternatives required a definite need to not be seen by the hostiles. The first choice could give the Indians an escape route to the east if being attacked from the south. The second choice gave General Crook's command probably holding the south avenue of escape and LTC. Custer not allowing the Indians an east escape route.

LTC. Custer needed to get closer to the Little Big Horn, following the main trail so to get up-front information to the exact location of the Indian encampment. Then, Custer could formulate his plan of attack keeping with a timetable allowing for Gibbon - Terry to be in a supporting position, to keep the Indians from scattering. This plan would not be a coordinated effort, but a good possibility and keeping in the spirit of General Terry's orders. LTC. Custer knew that Gibbon - Terry would be at the north end of the Little Big Horn on the 26th of June so he could try to arrange his attack the same day.

While the column was leaving Busby at approximately 11:00 P.M., LT. Varnum and his scouts were already well out in advance, heading toward the hilltop called the "Crows Nest" along the Rosebud divide and reached it approximately 2:00 A.M. Later the same morning, on the 25th of June, Custer went to the "Crows Nest" for approximately 1 hour, overlooking Reno Creek and supposedly into the Little Big Horn valley about 15 miles away. At this time, LTC. Custer was told by the guide, Fred Gerard, Crow scouts and some Ree scouts that they could see where the hostile village was located along the Little Big Horn valley. Mitch Boyer told LTC. Custer of the size of the encampment. Custer did not see this himself, but did put some thought to it and later told his officers that he did <u>not</u> believe it.

LT. Hare heard Mitch Boyer tell LTC. Custer "General, I have been with these Indians for 30 years and this is the largest village I have ever heard of." The scouts repeatedly told Custer of this fact, but size was not what worried him. His overriding concern was that the Lakota and Cheyenne would break up and scatter. The scouts also tried to tell Custer that if the village was surprised, the warriors would fight desperately to protect the women and children.

Now, LTC. Custer was informed by George Herendeen and Mitch Boyer that the soldiers were seen by mounted hostile Indians. He was then informed by LT. Cooke and CPT. Tom Custer that the hostile Indians found some packs that had fallen off the pack mules. LTC. Custer here decided to continue on toward the Little Big Horn valley and told his officers that "we will press on as quickly as we are able and attack the village if possible." The idea was that the hostiles would not stand against a whole regiment of cavalry and as soon as the Indians heard of the cavalry advance, they would try to get away from them. In all of the previous experiences, when the immediate presence of troops were known to the hostiles, they resorted to all kinds of ruses to mislead the troops to delay the soldiers' advance toward their encampment and to allow the squaws and children time to run and scatter. Time now has become paramount. Because of what LTC. Custer knew of the Indians, two elements in his thinking and planning were: surprise and speed. Surprise may have been already compromised, therefore, speed was most important.

So at this time of LTC. Custer's advance from the Rosebud divide toward the Little Big Horn valley, his regiment was proceeding as a reconnaissance in force, due to the fact that there was no definite target and no definite target location. All Custer knew at this time was that there were many hostile Indians somewhere to the west of his position. LTC. Custer also knew that he had to know the full picture of his target, both the size of the village and the number of villages, if appropriate, (a lesson he learned at the Washita battle). Custer was not concerned about the number of Indians.

At the Rosebud divide, LTC. Custer assigned his twelve companies into four respective battalions, each commanded by one of four senior officers. Captain Benteen's battalion was ordered by LTC. Custer to advance to the left front and recon that terrain for hostile Indians and "to pitch into anything he came across". LTC. Custer was providing his regiment left flank security and possibly determine if there were hostiles to the south and west along Reno Creek into the Little Big Horn valley. Custer wanted all of the hostiles ahead of him. The hills that were 3 or 4 miles to the south, needed to be checked and then LTC. Custer notified of any hostiles. LTC. Custer rendered this mission valid and necessary for reconnaissance purposes. (see map 6, appendix 1) This movement at this time was questionable. Custer could have waited until he was closer to the Little Big Horn valley, when he might have more intelligence available and to insure a more cohesive main body, before sending CPT. Benteen off. At this point, LTC. Custer could have easily and effectively sent his Ree Indian scouts to check this area out first and if necessary, then dispatch CPT. Benteen if there were Indians there. By LTC. Custer sending CPT. Benteen with his battalion (25% of the total strength) to scout for the hostiles south and west of the Little Big Horn valley, Custer was losing control of Benteen for a considerable amount of time and possibly for good. LTC. Custer had to consider it to be an independent fighting force and presumed that CPT. Benteen would prevail over any Indian obstacle, also assuming that he (Custer) would not need Benteen's battalion. The area of CPT. Benteen's reconnaissance was about 60 square miles. LTC. Custer already knew that he had enough Indians to contend with, again according to his Crow scouts, and now Custer lost the advantage of having an additional full battalion available for his immediate needs; for example, a reserve, which is very important in military operations. Almost all military operations command a reserve, either offensively or defensively and the Little Big Horn Battle proved that LTC. Custer needed CPT. Benteen's battalion closer to his force to be effective.

On the morning of June 25, 1876, LTC. Custer's decision to move to the Little Big Horn River from his regiment's location at the Rosebud divide, was based on his knowledge that the Lakota and Cheyenne had seen the regiment's encampment. At this time, the element of surprise seemed to be lost and the only advantage left was time. The time to reach the Little Big Horn valley, the assumed location of the Indians, as shown by their sign and the belief of the regiment's Crow and Ree scout's reports. LTC. Custer was obsessed with the U.S. Army's extant that the plains Indians would not stand and fight, that they would run and scatter and that they were inferior to the superior U.S. forces. Even General Terry believed that either of his commands could alone subdue the Indians, regardless of their numbers. This obsession was the root cause for Custer's decisions during the battle of the Little Big Horn.

LTC. Custer's move west on Reno Creek was fast paced. (see map 6, appendix 1) His intention was speed. The rising dust in the distance brought attention to Custer and his scouts. Half Yellow Face, George Herendeen, LT. Hare and Fred Gerard confirmed this sighting of rising dust. Then, Gerard spotted Indians ahead fleeing and told Custer "There go your Indians running like devils." There were about fifty of them.

This is when LTC. Custer gave the order to Major Reno to advance and subdue the fleeing Indians, through LT. Cooke who told MAJ. Reno "the Indians are 2 1/2 miles ahead and you should go as fast as is prudent and to charge them wherever they went and we will support you." LTC. Custer sent MAJ. Reno and his battalion of three companies (another 25% of his regimental strength) to attack or subdue the fleeing Indians in Reno Valley, which were heading west toward the Little Big Horn River. LTC. Custer said he would support MAJ. Reno. At this time, Custer did not know to which direction the Indians would go after crossing the Little Big Horn River with Reno following. Launching MAJ. Reno against a target of only a few Indians and to pursue them wherever they went and attack was a commitment for action wherever they went - southward, westward or northward. LTC. Custer did not know where this attack would end up, therefore the only way that Custer could give Reno support was from the rear. LTC. Custer revealed that for the time being, MAJ. Reno's battalion was taking care of itself against whatever it encountered, the same as CPT. Benteen's battalion on its scout.

This is one key to unlocking much of the mystery surrounding LTC. Custer's thinking and tactics at the Little Big Horn, the true premises.

1. Custer did not know there was a very large Indian village to the northwest just beyond the bluffs.

2. Custer did not know that it was the only hostile Indian village.

3. Custer did not know that he could turn north from Reno Creek and perform a flank attack in support of Reno's attack of the moving Indians.

4. Custer did not give orders to Reno to attack the large Indian village in the Little Big Horn valley.

CHAPTER 4:

"CUSTER'S RECONNAISSANCE"

<u>From this point, LTC. Custer's movements on the battlefield was an</u>
<u>intelligence gathering mission prior to an anticipated attack.</u> LTC.
Custer was forced to improvise on the run for lack of precise intelligence
and under the time pressure he was feeling, he feared the Indians would
flee. This was typical Custer. He was thinking, planning and devising
rapidly. It was important that he knew what was happening.

LTC. Custer, after sending MAJ. Reno to attack the fleeing Indians
on Reno Creek, moved northwest and watered his horses. (see map 3,
appendix 1) Mitch Boyer and his four Crow scouts leaves Custer's
command and heads up the bluffs on the east side of the Little Big
Horn River. LTC. Custer, all on his own premonition and prior to
receiving Fred Gerard's report of the Indians confronting MAJ. Reno,
through LT. Cooke, begins to mount the bluffs and is seen by a number
of Reno's troops, who were moving down the Little Big Horn valley.

Fred Gerard got across the Little Big Horn River and one of his
Ree scouts called out that the hostile Indians were coming out to meet
Reno. Gerard claimed "Hell, Custer ought to know this right away, for
he (Custer) thinks that the Indians were running. Custer ought to know
that they are preparing to fight. I'll go back and inform him." Gerard
went back toward Custer and met LT. Cooke at the knoll, 1/2 or 3/4 of
a mile east of Ford A. LT. Cooke heard from Fred Gerard that the
Indians were coming up the valley in large numbers and the Adjutant
responded "All right, I'll go back and report it to Custer."

LTC. Custer must have felt that it was a delaying action by the warriors to allow the families to flee to safety. {note: Custer believed Gerard, but Gerard only related the findings from what the Ree scouts said they saw, which from a long distance in dust clouds, may have been possibly wrong or just what the Rees wanted to say to stay out of the fight.} But LT. Cooke's report confirmed LTC. Custer's worst fear (obsession) that he arrived too late for a complete surprise and this intelligence received from Fred Gerard reinforced his decision to continue to the high ground. LTC. Custer's command continues to mount the bluffs more inland, than Custer himself, who stays along the bluff's ledge to get to Reno Hill. (see map 3, appendix 1) LTC. Custer's scout, Mitch Boyer, and the four Crow scouts are at the edge of the bluffs on Reno Hill where Custer will join them.* LT. Varnum sees the Company E Greyhorse unit on the bluffs from his view from the Little Big Horn valley.

LTC. Custer was a front commander. He had to know and see what was out ahead so he could determine his next moves. The east bluffs of the Little Big Horn River were the perfect spots to get this overview. LTC. Custer did not slow down until he reached the high ground of Reno Hill at 1:40 P.M. He could see the massive amount of dust in front of the village and could see MAJ. Reno's battalion moving north toward it. Reno was doing his job of dealing with the Indians to his front, and by sheer coincidence, MAJ. Reno was moving north toward the Lakota and Cheyenne encampment. (see appendix 2)

While this ridgeline where LTC. Custer viewed the valley was high, it did not let him get a good view of the camp's lower end. Mitch Boyer and his four Crow scouts, Goes Ahead, White Man Runs Him, Hairy Moccasin and Curly, are now told by Custer to head north along the bluffs to Weir Point. (see map 3, appendix 1)

LTC. Custer moved north along the bluff about 1/4 of a mile to elevation point 3411 and again saw Reno's men, plus had a little better view of the village, the time being 1:50 P.M. Since MAJ. Reno was moving in the right direction and the village appeared larger than anticipated - all of which LTC. Custer saw from 3411 - Custer had to be satisfied with seeing MAJ. Reno's men on the skirmish line and the Indians keeping their distance. This gave time for Custer to advance north and bag the non-combatants that were fleeing. The refugees had to be dealt with and separately forcing Custer to improvise on the run, because of the lack of precise intelligence and the time pressure. He, therefore, needed the high ground north to find the real answers for what must be done to prevent the Indians from escaping. With MAJ. Reno successfully engaged with the Indians, LTC. Custer now needed to go further downsteam and he needed to go there fast.

* LTC. Custer with two others are seen at elevation point 3411 by LT. De Rudio in the valley. Custer leaves 3411 at 1:55 P.M. and moves to Cedar Coulee to join his command, having seen Reno dismounted and holding against the Indians. (PVT. Martini confirms) (see map 3, appendix 1) The next high point downstream was Weir Point, but the terrain was not favorable and it was too close to elevation point 3411. Therefore, heading to Weir Point from 3411 would not be an advantage. LTC. Custer could seek high ground much further downriver and be much closer to his enemy and the current situation.

It is evident from the Indian reactions during the first ten minutes of battle that the 7th U.S. Cavalry had surprised the encampment. Their words and actions belie any assertion that LTC. Custer had walked into an ambush. The Indians fought General Crook on the 17th of June in an action 20 miles from their village. They didn't want soldiers approaching their encampment. If any warning of Custer did come to the Indians, it was on such short notice that no effective countermeasures could have been taken before MAJ. Reno's battalion attacked the roving Indians on Reno Creek.

** The Indian actions in this early segment of the battle, show that the encampment was surprised. In the Indian village there was turmoil and excitement. Warriors were looking to the safety of their families. Many heard the alarm, but didn't believe it; then the warriors had to run to find their horses. Numerous Indians said that the arrival of the 7th U.S. Cavalry was unexpected.

** Let's take a look at the size of the Indian encampment. (see map 4, appendix 1) The soldiers did not have the total vision of the camp, because it was wooded terrain intervening with bluffs and had a lot of smoke and dust prevalent in the air. They assumed from the start that the encampment was very large. After losing the battle, the encampment became astronomically huge to the survivors of the 7th U.S. Cavalry. The actual size of the village occupied on the 25th of June during the battle was much smaller than the terrain showed on the morning of the 27th of June, when the Montana column reached it, because a large number of Indians relocated just north during the evening of June 25th for various reasons. Through the years, there have been numerous estimates as to the number of Indians and warriors, the high percentage of these were totally over guessed, i.e. 12,000 Indians, 4,000 warriors in a village 4 miles long and 1 1/2 miles wide and had 2,000 lodges (tipis). The Native Americans, Lakota and Cheyenne, gave their estimates not in miles, but by actual terrain placement. They said the encampment went from Medicine Tail Coulee to the first large turn west in the Little Big Horn River upstream, and only as wide as a short walk from the west to the river. Putting this in miles was a village 1 1/2 miles long and about 300 yards wide, for a combined 1/4 to 1/3 square miles, with 1000 warriors. The number of lodges was not mentioned.

LTC. Custer needed to find more information about the actual length of the village and the terrain in order to overtake and subdue the fleeing Indian encampment. So, Custer's five companies headed down Cedar Coulee toward the Medicine Tail Coulee, which led to the Little Big Horn River at 2:05 P.M. (see maps 3, 4 - appendix 1) LTC. Custer was now on his own. MAJ. Reno was on his own. At this time, 2:05 P.M., Custer sent a message to CPT. Benteen to come to him with ammo packs, not to Reno, through Trumpeter Martini as the messenger.

From this point in the Little Big Horn battle, the only information about LTC. Custer's movements came from Indian sources, archeology and where the dead bodies of the troopers lay, plus some horse trails.

LTC. Custer was now maneuvering his five companies without knowing of Reno's tragic retreat at 2:25 P.M. LTC. Custer could not and did not militarily forsee MAJ. Reno's retreat.

The number of Indians did not come under consideration, even though the village was enormous, and LTC. Custer had no worry but one, that the Indians would run and flee from the troops. His job now was to head them off from the north end of the encampment, but he needed to go further downstream to the high ground to make a plan and find a crossing over the Little Big Horn River and await CPT. Benteen's battalion.

* Mitch Boyer releases his Crow scouts and moves off Weir Point to join LTC. Custer, who is descending Cedar Coulee and heading for Medicine Tail Coulee. Three Crows confirm this - White Man Runs Him, Goes Ahead and Hairy Moccasin. (see map 3, appendix 1)* Mitch Boyer leaves Weir Point at 2:10 P.M. before Reno retreats.

** Gall and Iron Cedar watch Custer move into Medicine Tail Coulee from the bluffs on the east side of the Little Big Horn River.

* Some Ree Indian scouts captured a number of ponies in the valley and made their way up the bluffs. Near the top, they passed the rear of LTC. Custer's column, which was beginning it's journey down Cedar Coulee. The Rees were Red Star, Strikes Two, Little Sioux, Boy Chief, One Bull, Bull Stands in the Water and Dakota Whole Buffalo.

* The three Crows, Goes Ahead, Hairy Moccasin and White Man Runs Him, from their view north of Weir Point along the Little Big Horn River bluffs, can see LTC. Custer's command ascending the hills to the east toward Luce Ridge at 2:35 P.M. (see map 5, appendix 1)

The 7th U.S. Cavalry, or part of it, after reaching Medicine Tail Coulee could have easily ascended the East Ridge hillside and possibly could have seen CPT. Benteen's battalion moving from the Little Big Horn up to Reno Hill. This would have been a tremendous advantage for LTC. Custer to have had this information. They would only have had interest in ascending East Ridge for informational purposes of who was behind them to the east or south, since the most likely route in the flow of movement north would be Luce Ridge, in order to get more positive information on the village and get closer to it.

LTC. Custer with his five companies was still on a reconnaissance and alone. He was not planning to attack the village. At this time, he had only 42% of his command strength. LTC. Custer reached Luce

Ridge at 2:40 P.M. and found out from his brother, Boston - riding forward from the pack train - that CPT. Benteen was on the main trail.

Messenger Martini and Boston Custer met each other passing on the trail on or about the Reno Hill vicinity at 2:20 P.M., before Reno's retreat. The conversation most likely, since they both were in a hurry, was very brief, with Boston saying to Martini that CPT. Benteen was just back down the hill on Reno Creek and Martini pointing to the trail down Cedar Coulee to the right, as to where LTC. Custer went.

It is doubtful that after the short halt that Boston Custer would have gone to the left and gotten near enough to the edge of the bluffs to have seen any action involving MAJ. Reno and his retreat, since Cedar Coulee was to the right. So he could not have told LTC. Custer anything except where CPT. Benteen was located on the trail, which would have been good news to LTC. Custer if he maybe hadn't already received that information from some of his troops that passed over East Ridge.

** White Bull, from the bluffs on the east side of the river, saw troopers on the hills moving north just about at East Ridge to Luce Ridge. Runs the Enemy, Short Bull and Flying Hawk also saw this movement of troops. (see map 5, appendix 1)

** One Bull, Red Feather and Fears Nothing saw CPT. Benteen's battalion reaching the beginning of the hilltops. (Reno Hill) (see map 6, appendix 1)

From here, LTC. Custer continued north, based on his obsession, to find a crossing over the Little Big Horn River. At this point, LTC. Custer irrevocably detached his immediate command of five companies from the rest of his regiment.

From Luce Ridge, LTC. Custer most likely again saw the Indian encampment and the dust clouds pertaining to movement in the village, but he needed to get closer yet before making future decisions. Here Custer sent a unit of his command down the ridge adjacent to Medicine Tail Coulee to check out the possibility of using the ford at the junction of Medicine Tail Coulee and the Little Big Horn River and also wanting to see the village closer for information as to its size, not visible from Luce Ridge. Custer did not want to attack the middle of the village. The move of the troops to the Little Big Horn River at Medicine Tail Coulee (Ford B), definitely was not for attack, there were only two troops. Custer left the other battalion on Luce Ridge. (see map 5, appendix 1)

** Now that Custer's troops were seen by the Lakota that had been climbing the east bluffs of the Little Big Horn to give Reno combat, began to head toward the north to meet Custer. The number of Indians vacating the Reno fight were many, most going north through the village. White Bull, One Bull, Fears Nothing, Runs the Enemy, Flying Hawk, Short Bull, Crazy Horse, Two Moon and Shave Elk are a few of those Indians leaving the Reno fight and heading for the Custer column.

At the Rosebud divide, when LTC. Custer had assigned the companies of his command to the ranking officers into four battalions, he kept the Keogh and Yates battalions with him as he moved north from Reno Creek. Custer being a front leader, most probably accompanied the battalion that went toward the river at Ford B, but he could have stayed with CPT. Keogh. LT. Algernon Smith with Company E, the Greyhorse troop, headed down along the upper side of Medicine Tail Coulee in full view of the Indians, while Custer was accompanying Captain Yates, the battalion and Company F commander, headed to Custer's bluff at the lower part of the Luce-Nye Cartwright slope. CPT. Keogh's battalion (Companies I, L, C) stayed at Luce Ridge. (see map 5, appendix 1)

LTC. Custer and his five companies, by staying on the high ground to be easily seen by the Lakota and Cheyenne, were giving relief to MAJ. Reno's command at the south end of the village by diverting the hostiles' attention to them, still not knowing of MAJ. Reno's retreat.

** Oglala warrior Shave Elk and several other hostiles that were moving up Medicine Tail Coulee, ran into Company E and turned back to Ford B.

LTC. Custer and Captain Yates' Company F arrive at the bluff (Custer's bluff) overlooking Ford B, about 1/5 of a mile from the river at 2:55 P.M. LT. Smith's Company E arrives a little closer to Ford B and deploys his men both mounted and dismounted. (see map 5, appendix 1)

** Lights said that they got within one-quarter of a mile of the ford and "That was as near as they (troops) ever got to the river".

It is also corroborated by Indian testimony recognizing Company E's grey horses being the ones toward the river. Some hostiles, most likely Cheyenne, since their camp was directly on the west side of the river at Ford B, crossed the river and harassed Company E. The Cheyenne were over to the east side before the troops had a chance to cross.

** Bob Tail Horse, Yellow Nose, Antelope, Two Moon, Lights, Red Hawk, Eagle Elk, Fears Nothing, Lone Bear and American Horse all stated in their own words that LTC. Custer's troops came down from the northeast Nye-Cartwright Ridge to Ford B. (see map 5, appendix 1)

** Hollow Horn Bear said that there was no fighting at the ford, just sporadic long-range firing. Soldiers fired into the village and no one was hit. He did not think the soldiers wanted to come into the village since a lot of warriors were gathering.

At the ford, CPT. Yates with Company F and LTC. Custer having seen what he wanted to see, which did not include the use of Ford B as a crossing point, turned and retrograded back up the steep hill to the Nye-Cartwright Ridge at 3:05 P.M., with LT. Smith's Company E acting as rear guard for the battalion. (see map 5, appendix 1)

CPT. Keogh, at Luce Ridge, sees hostile Indians coming down Medicine Tail Coulee from the bluffs on the east side of the Little Big Horn River. Keogh opens fire on them (the Wolf Tooth and Big Foot bands) to protect Company E's left flank. Then Company E pulls back and follows Company F back up the hill to Nye-Cartwright Ridge, following proper retrograde protocol.

** Tall Bull, Yellow Nose, Waterman, Two Moon, Ice, Shave Elk, Red Hawk and Hump all stated in their own words that the troops at Ford B retreated back up the hill to Nye-Cartwright Ridge, slowly. None of the Indians said that the soldiers went up Greasy Grass to Calhoun Hill.

CPT. Keogh with his battalion mounts up and also heads north from Luce Ridge to Nye-Cartwright Ridge, about 1/4 of a mile distance. Keogh's battalion continues to fire on the harassing Indian encroachment and sets up a mounted skirmish line when he reaches Nye-Cartwright Ridge at 3:10 P.M. The Lakota and Cheyenne now are crossing to the east side of the Little Big Horn River and they see all of LTC. Custer's five companies together on Nye-Cartwright Ridge. Now Custer starts moving his troops north directly to Calhoun Hill. (see map 5, appendix 1)

** Standing Bear, He Dog, Wolf Tooth and Good Voiced Elk all said that the cavalry moved together, united, riding to Calhoun Hill. The Indians saw this with their own eyes and their narratives were simple in meaning.

LTC. Custer at this time, 3:20 P.M., left the Keogh battalion of Companies C, I and L in a holding action on Calhoun Hill as a reserve and to await CPT. Benteen. (see maps 5, 7 - appendix 1) LTC. Custer, with CPT. Yates' battalion of Companies E & F, continued north along the battle ridge on the reverse side (east side), still on a reconnaissance to find a route to a crossing over the Little Big Horn River to collect the non-combatants, who were northwest of Ford B heading for Squaw/Chasing Creek.

** The Lakota and Cheyenne were not dormant. They were in large numbers crossing the Little Big Horn River to the east side and moving up the slopes, gullies and coulees to meet the 7th U.S. Cavalry. They moved stealthily up Deep Coulee to the south and east of Calhoun Hill, they moved up Greasy Grass toward Findley Ridge west of Calhoun Hill and moved up Greasy Grass east and northeast toward battle ridge. The Indians, in their familiar preferred terrain, were beginning to consolidate in mass for a large scale fight at Calhoun Hill.

** Wolf Tooth, White Bull, Red Feather, Runs the Enemy and Hump are a very small number giving the information just mentioned. There were many other Lakota and Cheyenne that gave the same testimony. (see map 7, appendix 1)

CPT. Keogh's battalion was spread out on the south end of battle ridge with Company L on Calhoun Hill, Company C in the center and Company I on the north end about at the middle of battle ridge. Keogh had approximately 120 men to cover 1/2 of a mile, both the west and east side of battle ridge. This was definitely a holding action awaiting CPT. Benteen or new orders from LTC. Custer. A defense was out of the question.

** Two Moons said that LTC. Custer went behind the Monument Hill and went down into the valley.

LTC. Custer was making his reconnaissance northwest, leaving Company E between the north end of battle ridge and Cemetery Ridge. He, along with CPT. Yates' Company F, continued northwest toward the Little Big Horn River and a hopeful ford on the north end of the Cheyenne encampment, arriving at 3:45 P.M. (see map 7, appendix 1)

** Two Moon and Wolf Tooth saw Company E and Company F make this movement, noticing the difference of the troops by the color of their horses.

LTC. Custer and Company F returned to Cemetery Ridge after having been to the Little Big Horn River and supposedly seeing a crossing ford. (see map 7, appendix 1)

** Cheyenne historian, John Stands In Timber, said that soldiers approaching a far northern crossing were fired upon and retreated. That a soldier was shot from his horse, but was taken by another soldier as they were driven back by Indians coming out of the Little Big Horn River tree lines. The soldiers went back to the cemetery grounds. White Cow Bull and Cheyenne Hanging Wolf corroborated this.

At Cemetery Ridge, LTC. Custer just halted and waited. His reconnaissance was finally over at 3:55 P.M. Most likely, he was expecting the CPT. Keogh and CPT. Benteen battalions to show up soon to his position so he could start an offensive movement to engage the Lakota and Cheyenne women, children and elderly, located at

Squaw/Chasing Creek across from Ford D, in order to force the warriors to subside with their fighting. (see map 7, appendix 1)

CPT. Benteen's men, after arriving on the Reno hilltop just after 3:05 P.M., set up a skirmish line and began to chase off the nearby hostiles also on the high ground. The troopers returned about 3:20 P.M.

LT. Hare, after being sent to the pack train to get some ammunition pack mules, returned to Reno Hill with them at about 3:45 P.M. CPT. Benteen, in following with LTC. Custer's demand for CPT. Benteen and the ammunition pack mules to come to him, could not have started to LTC. Custer from Reno Hill until about 3:55 P.M. At this time, LTC. Custer was at Cemetery Hill waiting for the arrival of the Benteen and Keogh battalions. This was a four mile distance and CPT. Benteen's battalion could never have made it to LTC. Custer in time, especially having to fight through 800 Native American Lakota and Cheyenne to get to him.

LTC. Custer was looking at his regiment with 11 of 12 companies in an offensive posture. He had MAJ. Reno's 3 companies holding the south end of the village and he (Custer) with CPT. Yates' 2 companies, CPT. Keogh's 3 companies and CPT. Benteen with his 3 companies, all together attacking the Lakota and Cheyenne encampment from the north over Ford D at the Little Big Horn River, constituting a pincer movement to collect the hostiles.

LTC. Custer was on a reconnaissance since he left the Rosebud divide. The only offensive action was when MAJ. Reno was ordered to attack the band of Indians along Reno Creek and follow them wherever they went. Reno was not told to attack the unknown village from the south, although it coincidentally looked like that happened when the roving band turned north when they got on the west side of the Little Big Horn River, with Reno following.

The LTC. Custer mindset never thought that MAJ. Reno would be overcome and had retreated from battle. Custer also could not have seen CPT. Benteen being halted by MAJ. Reno and stopping to help. This unfortunate incident, the routed retreat by Reno and getting between Benteen and Custer, was another nail in the coffin for the collapse of the Regiment and the Indian Expeditionary Force mission, as Custer awaited the additional troops at Cemetery Ridge to begin the attack.

LTC. Custer's mistake of incorrectly estimating the resolve of his Native American foe and their fighting abilities along with having an entrenched extant of the plains Indians that they would not fight, but run and scatter, allowed him to continue a reconnaissance without realizing the total deficiency of this maneuver and allowing for no mutual combat support of his battalions. Had LTC. Custer been fighting another foe, other than the Lakota and Cheyenne plains Indians, he would never have allowed this scenario to happen.

CHAPTER 5:

"CUSTER'S "5" COMPANY FIGHT"

LTC. Custer was obsessed about finding that northern crossing and had not concerned himself with the massive encroachment of Lakota and Cheyenne warriors toward his position.

LTC. Custer's five companies, with a total of 210 men, were now spread out about a mile in not good defensible terrain and were not in mutual support of each other. The Native American Lakota and Cheyenne, estimated about 800 warriors, have been infiltrating around the 7th U.S. Cavalry in terrain very favorable to the Indian type of fighting. The cavalrymen, without the advantage of using combined mounted cavalry tactics, were now reduced to fighting as infantrymen without the experience. There were no military maneuvers. They were now only reacting to Indian initiatives and the numerical difference in troopers to warriors was not at all even. The outcome was inevitable with close combat being the factor.

The Indian narratives of the Custer five company battle, as explained by the Lakota and Cheyenne warriors who fought against the 7th U.S. Cavalry, give an accurate account of what happened. While LTC. Custer was still on his reconnaissance toward the northern end of the Lakota and Cheyenne encampment looking for a crossing over the Little Big Horn River, CPT. Keogh's battalion was being enveloped by the warriors and firing had already started at long range. The main avenue the Indians used to engage the soldiers on Calhoun Hill was Deep Coulee, which came up from the west at Ford B and by-passed the base of Calhoun Hill around to the east side of battle ridge. There were two other infiltration routes the Indians took. The first was up Greasy Grass Ridge toward Findley Ridge. The second was Calhoun Coulee, a spur of Deep Ravine on the left of Greasy Grass Ridge to Calhoun Hill. These last two infiltration routes were, most likely, the ones that Company C, commanded by LT. Harrington (CPT. Tom Custer's second in command), was sent by CPT. Keogh to plug the gap to the Indians advancing on Calhoun Hill. (see map 8, appendix 1)

** Two Eagles, Fears Nothing, Red Hawk and Tall Bull verified the movement to these positions by the troops.

The infiltration of the Native Americans, virtually surrounding the five companies of the 7th U.S. Cavalry, was the catalyst to its eventual demise. Not only was the Keogh battalion being surrounded and pressed by numerous Lakota and Cheyenne on the center and south end of battle ridge and Calhoun Hill, but now Yates' battalion, on the north end, was having a similar problem. The Indians were advancing around them from the west, following the route that LTC. Custer had taken from Ford D through Cemetery Ridge and also swinging around to the north side of Custer Hill. (see map 9, appendix 1) The Indians moving up from Ford B on Greasy Grass Ridge, including Deep Ravine, were threatening CPT. Yates from the south, southwest direction.

** Company E, from it's position on Custer Hill, moved south toward Deep Ravine to check the Indian advance toward the northeast and Company F's flank. The Indians withdrew for a short time.

** Wolf Tooth was leading a band of warriors here and mentioned this movement of troops. This also drove Wooden Leg out of Deep Ravine and was witnessed by Antelope.

The 7th U.S. Cavalry at this point, countering the Lakota and Cheyenne initiatives, did not support an actual defensive perimeter. Custer was thinking offensively. The soldiers were too few to command a proper defensive posture against all the directions that the infiltrating Indians were coming from. LTC. Custer never thought or intended to be in this position while awaiting CPT. Benteen; therefore, it was too late to coordinate a defense with CPT. Yates' battalion and let alone, one including CPT. Keogh's battalion. There was not the advantage of having a communication coordination. Both CPT. Yates and CPT. Keogh were too involved with their own problems to even think that LTC. Custer could attempt that tactic to combine their units, plus there were just a few Indians in between their respective battalions.

With the loss of men, having wounded to protect and having most of the horses scared away, the 7th U.S. Cavalry were immobilized at their present positions, with no chance to retreat. They most likely were also low on ammunition with having their reserve ammunition left on the horses that had been run off by the noise of firearms or by the Indians spooking them with blanket waving.

** Standing Bear, Eagle Elk and Flying By were involved with this last activity of stampeding cavalry horses.

On both the northern and southern flanks of the 7th U.S. Cavalry's stand on battle ridge, the Native Americans were having their way. The big events were now unfolding and all were in favor of the Lakota and Cheyenne.

** On the north end, Lame White Man and his warriors attacked Company E between Cemetery Ravine and Deep Ravine and pushed them back to Custer Hill.

** Company F was also attacked on the cemetery grounds and was driven back up the hill to Monument Hill at 4:15 P.M., attested to by Rain in the Face.

In the center of the 7th U.S. Cavalry's occupied terrain, Company I was on the east, or reverse side, of battle ridge.

** Crazy Horse and White Bull lead a daring attack with glory rides severing the line of Companies C and I. While in the south, the Indians triumpfully attacked a detachment of Company C on Findley Ridge and Company L on Calhoun Hill. (see maps 8, 9 - appendix 1)

** The fighting was not hand to hand, but the Indians totally surrounded the troopers, even getting between their positions. Almost all of the fighting was from a reasonable distance behind protected terrain features.

After these above notable attacks by the Native Americans, the soldiers still alive made efforts to reach the next company to their north, and the last being Company F on Custer Hill. There were a few troopers to make their temporary escape to Custer Hill from Companies L, C and I, but most were cut down by the Indians. Some of the troopers were killed just fleeing in whatever direction. The Native Americans fought as individuals, but sometimes joining some other Indians, such as those who were together at the Henryville site. They were firing a good number of Henry repeating rifles on the soldiers at Findley Ridge and Calhoun Hill.

The 7th U.S. Cavalry's last stand on Custer Hill was not a sensational, dramatic, massive hand to hand battle. The Lakota and Cheyenne Native Americans fought just as they had been doing. Fighting from a protected distance. In the very end, some troopers were killed in close combat and some troopers were killed running away. (see map 9, appendix 1)

It should be noted that when this fight on Custer Hill was still going on, the 7th U.S. Cavalry battalions of Major Reno and Captain Benteen were seen on Weir Point by the Lakota and Cheyenne Native Americans. The time was 4:20 P.M.

** The Indians headed for the soldiers on Weir Point before the Custer fight on Monument Hill was concluded. Two of those Indians were Low Dog and Little Sun.

The fight on Custer Hill was over around 4:35 P.M.

My Final Conclusions

1. General Terry did not make long range reconnaissances of the target area prior to starting his operation which hindered a positive result for the 1876 Indian Expeditionary Force success.

2. General Terry did not use a single column reconnaissance task force while moving into the target area, thereby not having a coordinated attack on the hostiles; and by using a two column separate advance, that allowed the Lakota and Cheyenne to consolidate a force strong enough to defeat the column that came into contact with them first and alone.

3. General Terry did not use or listen to his valued scouts' knowledge and opinions for his Montana column movements, which ended up being too late to help the 7th U.S. Cavalry.

4. LTC. Custer in no way disobeyed General Terry's orders.

> a. George Herendeen failed to make his trip to the Montana column with the information about Tullock Creek, for whatever reason. LTC. Custer told him to go.

> b. LTC. Custer's move to the Little Big Horn from the Rosebud was within General Terry's spirit of orders for being in reasonable contact and awaiting overnight until attacking on June 26, 1876.

> c. LTC. Custer's move to the Little Big Horn from the Rosebud

divide was based on the fact that the 7th U.S. Cavalry was seen by actual hostiles, which required an action to proceed.

5. Scout George Herendeen failing to get the Tullock Creek information to General Terry was the probable cause for the Montana column's diversion across to the Big Horn River and the inevitable failure to get to the Little Big Horn River in the time expected, according to General Terry's Expedition plan.

6. LTC. Custer's move from the Rosebud divide to the Little Big Horn River was a reconnaissance in force and his movement from Reno Creek to the final battlefield was only a reconnaissance. He had no intentions of attacking the village until 11 of his 12 companies were in position.

7. LTC. Custer could have used his Ree scouts to make a reconnaissance of the area south of Reno Creek to the Little Big Horn valley, rather than give CPT. Benteen that assignment and instead keep Benteen's battalion close to the main body.

8. LTC. Custer sent MAJ. Reno to attack a small Indian force without knowing where they would end up.

9. LTC. Custer never attacked the village, neither did MAJ. Reno. They didn't know at that time of any Indian encampment.

10. LTC. Custer never knew of MAJ. Reno's disastrous retreat. He was expecting them to hold their ground.

11. MAJ. Reno's retreat was probably required to save his battalion, but the manner in which it was conducted was unspeakable. He failed to follow standard operating procedures for a military retrograde movement.

12. CPT. Benteen's interaction with MAJ. Reno's retreat was an unexpected circumstance. The battle with Custer in the north was already lost when CPT. Benteen, with ammo packs, would have attempted to fight through the Lakota and Cheyenne warriors to reach LTC. Custer and his "5" surrounded companies.

13. Had CPT. Benteen and MAJ. Reno tried to reach LTC. Custer and his five companies, with or without the pack train, the total 7th U.S. Cavalry would have been decimated by the Lakota and Cheyenne with the troops being caught and spaced out in the open in terrain favorable to a much larger foe.

14. LTC. Custer was really expecting CPT. Benteen to show up at his front position so he could begin his quest to subdue the Indian women, children and elderly.

15. LTC. Custer made no maneuvers in his battle, his sole mission was to get to the north end of the Indian encampment and having his regiment together engaging the non-combatants to stop any fighting of the Native American warriors.

16. LTC. Custer's reconnaissance mindset in conjunction with his extant belief of the Lakota and Cheyenne fighting abilities, did not allow him to see the Native Americans encroaching on his "5" company positions putting his spreadout troops in a no-defense, no-win situation.

MY FINAL STATEMENTS

My intentions were very simple. I just wanted to show the true facts, relate them to the events of the battle and allow the reader to make his/her opinions with the information given in this study. I have tried to not be biased about any of the participants in the Battle of the Little Big Horn and to only infer a better solution to an individual event if necessary.

Overall, I would say that the failure of the 1876 Indian Campaign and the partial extermination of the 7th U.S. Cavalry was a strategic error, both General Terry and LTC. Custer sharing equal responsibility. This was mainly due to the gross error of each underestimating the resolve and fighting ability of the Native American Lakota and Cheyenne Nations.

The Indians won in a fair fight!

APPENDIX 1

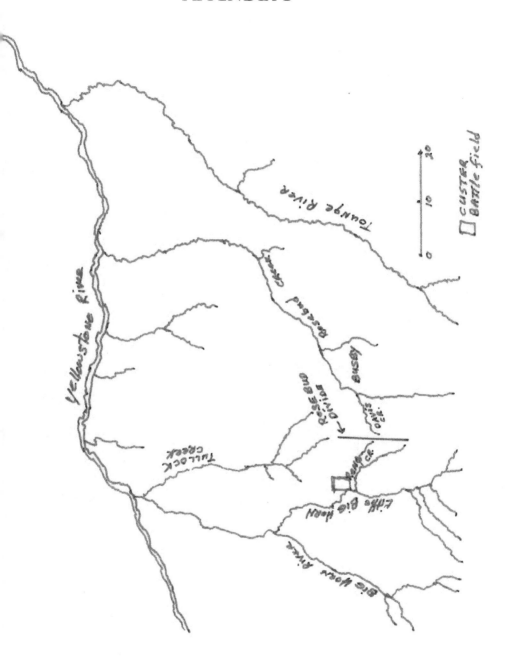

1. Expeditionary Force Target Area

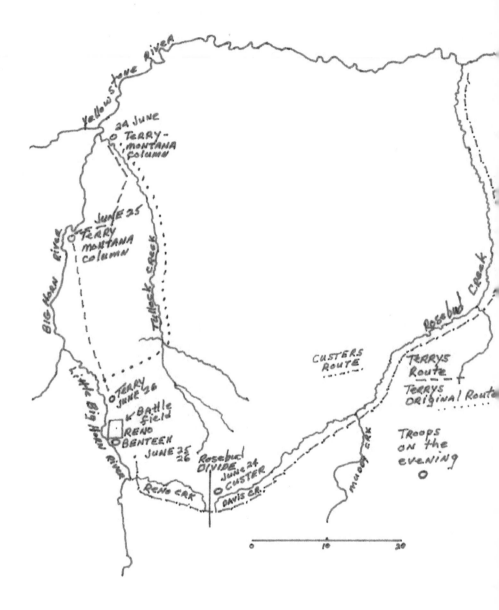

2. Montana and Custer Advance to the Little Big Horn

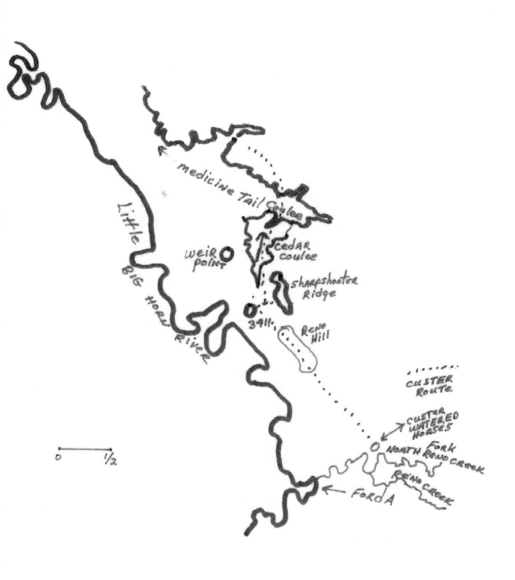

3. Custer's Reconnaissance

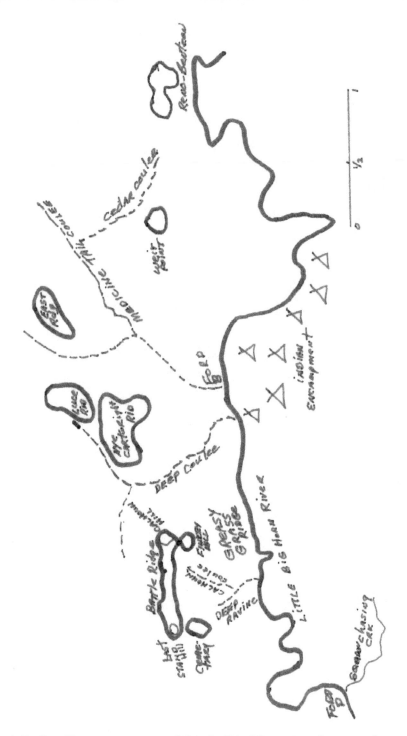

4. Indian Encampment and Little Big Horn Battleground

44

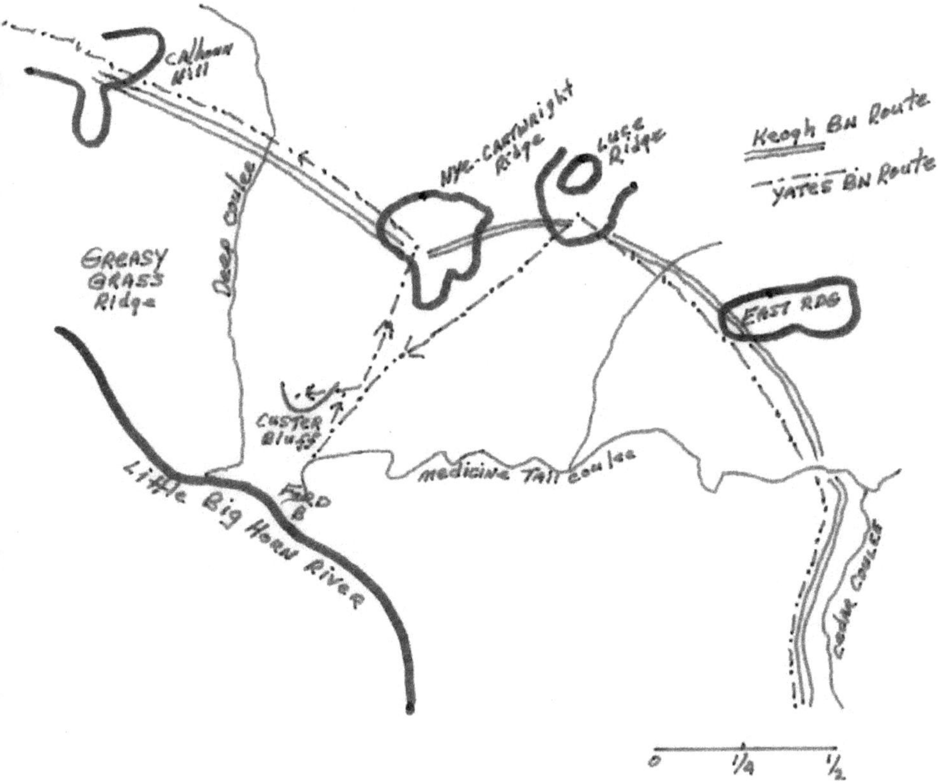
Calhoun Hill
Nye-Cartwright Ridge
Luce Ridge
Keogh Bn Route
Yates Bn Route
Greasy Grass Ridge
Deep Coulee
East Rdg
Custer Bluff
Ford B
Medicine Tail coulee
Little Big Horn River
Cedar Coulee
0
1/4
1/2

5. "5" Company Advance

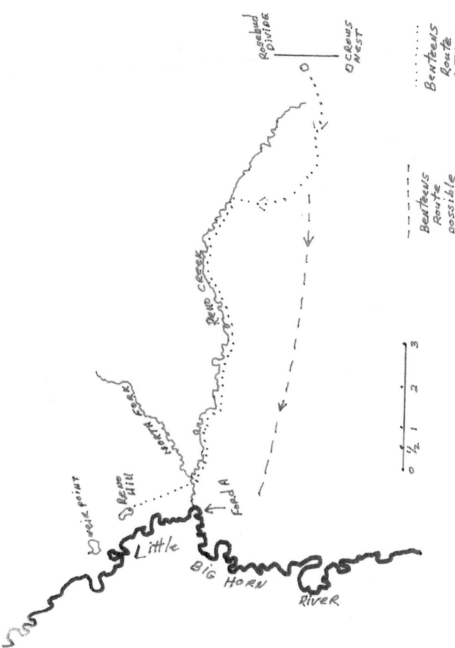

6. Benteen's Reconnaissance Route

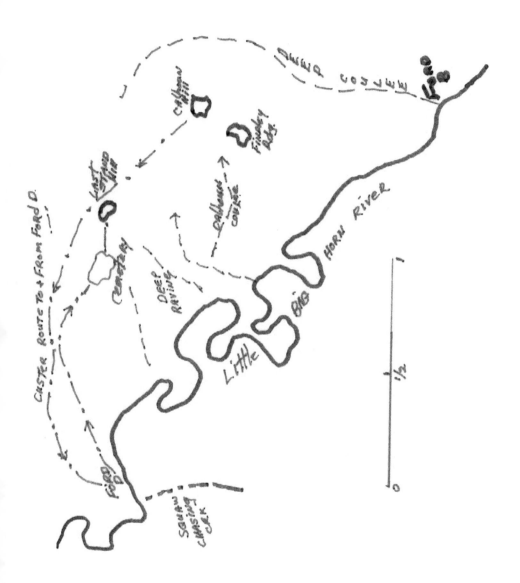

7. Yates and Custer Move Northwest

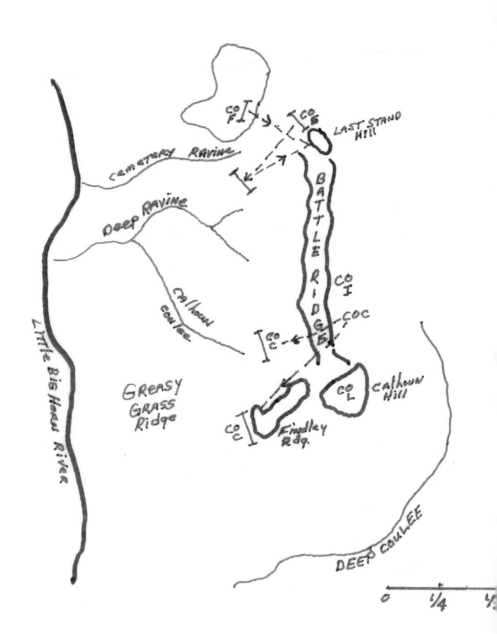

8. Yates and Keogh Positions

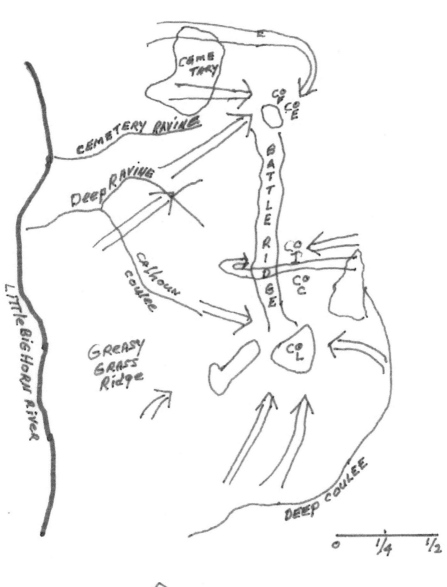

9. Indian Advances

APPENDIX 2

This is the route LTC. Custer took after leaving Reno Creek, watering the horses, then going to Reno Hill to overview the Little Big Horn valley. The times are based on the 7th U.S. Cavalry's departure at the Rosebud divide when LTC. Custer assigned his companies to the respective battalions. That time was 1200 noon on 25 June, 1876 and in accordance with LT. George Wallace's official time, him being the regiment's official itinerist. The approximate times entered in this appendix are based on the distance traveled and the rate of speed most likely taken by the horses in context with the urgency of the movement and the type of terrain encountered. Also, there were halt times included for viewing or waiting.

LOCATION	ARRIVAL TIME	DISTANCE IN MILES
RENO HILL	1:40	——
ELEVATION 3411	1:50	.25
CEDAR COULEE	2:05	.33
MEDICINE TAIL COULEE	2:25	.75
LUCE RIDGE	2:40	1.4
CUSTER BLUFF	2:55	.75
NYE-CARTWRIGHT RIDGE	3:07	.67
CALHOUN HILL	3:15	.86
MONUMENT HILL	By-Pass	.67
CEMETERY RIDGE	By-Pass	.25
FORD D	3:45	1.33
CEMETERY RIDGE	3:55	1.33
MONUMENT HILL	4:15	.25

APPENDIX 3

General Terry's written orders to LTC. Custer

Camp at Mouth of Rosebud River, Montana Territory
June 22d, 1876.
Lieutenant-Colonel Custer,
7th Cavalry

Colonel:
The Brigadier-General Commanding directs that,
as soon as your regiment can be made ready for the
march, you will proceed up the Rosebud in pursuit of
the Indians whose trail was discovered by Major Reno a
few days since. It is, of course, impossible to give you
any definite instructions in regard to this movement,
and were it not impossible to do so the Department
Commander places too much confidence in your zeal,
energy, and ability to wish to impose upon you precise
orders which might hamper your action when nearly in
contact with the enemy.

*He will, however, indicate to you his own views of
what your action should be, and he desires that you
should conform to them unless you shall see sufficient
reasons for departing from them. He thinks that you
should proceed up the Rosebud until you ascertain
definitely the direction in which the trail above spoken
of leads. Should it be found (as it appears almost
certain that it will be found) to turn towards the Little
Horn, he thinks that you should still proceed southward, perhaps as far as the headwaters of the Tongue,
and then turn towards the Little Horn, feeling constantly,
however, to your left, so as to preclude the possibility
of the escape of the Indians to the south or southeast by
passing around your left flank.*

*The column of Colonel Gibbon is now in motion for the
mouth of the Big Horn. As soon as it reaches that point
it will cross the Yellowstone and move up at least as far
as the forks of the Big and Little Horns. Of course its
future movements must be controlled by circumstances
as they arise, but it is hoped that the Indians, if upon
the Little Horn, may be so nearly inclosed by two
columns that their escape will be impossible.*

*The Department Commander desires that on your
way up the Rosebud you should thoroughly examine
the upper part of Tullock's Creek, and that you should
endeavor to send a scout through to Colonel Gibbon's
column, with information of the result of your
examination. The lower part of the creek will be examined
by a detachment from Colonel Gibbon's command.*

The supply steamer will be pushed up the Big Horn as far as the forks if the river is found to be navigable for that distance, and the Department Commander, who will accompany the column of Colonel Gibbon, desires you to report to him there not later than the expiration of the time for which your troops are rationed, unless in the meantime you receive further orders.

Very respectfully, your obedient servant,
E. W. Smith,
Captain 18th Infantry,
Acting Assistant Adjutant General.

CPSIA information can be obtained
at www.ICGtesting.com
Printed in the USA
LVHW081447091022
730293LV00013B/650